Cryptos of the Future

Investing In These Five Cryptocurrencies Could Make You a Fortune

Preface

Unless someone is under a rock for the entire previous decade, they would have heard the term cryptocurrency loud and clear. That is the impact these cryptos have created in less than ten years of their inception. Not just the people in the world of finance but individuals from various disciplines are watching the crypto space with a lot of interest. Hence, it is no wonder that cryptocurrencies are among the most spoken topics in the previous decade.

We need to know that there are numerous speculations in this area from the very beginning. Most of the experts have put forward their opinion on cryptos saying that it will change the face of the economy in the ways we can't imagine. However, a few of them believed that this entire phenomenon is just a bubble that may burst anytime soon. The latter opinion is ultimately proven wrong as the crypto industry is stronger than ever today than it was a few years ago.

It is a fact that this industry has made more millionaires in much less time than any other industry that we know. If not millionaires, many of the individuals are generating a consistent stream of income from cryptos by investing, trading, and mining them. We will be discussing each of these in the later sections of this book. According to crypto market experts, most of the cryptos in the market are undervalued according to their fundamental analysis.

Hence, this is the right time for us to identify & invest in the cryptos that have strong fundamentals but are undervalued. Investing in them now is one of the best financial decisions we could take as they may reap huge profits for us in the near future. But as we all know, education is crucial before investing in anything that we aren't entirely aware of. The purpose of this book is to give you that basic yet essential education in the simplest way possible.

Once you are clear on the basics, we will introduce you to the five high potential cryptocurrencies. We will perform both fundamental and technical analyses for these five coins so that you will know why we chose these five cryptos from a considerable lot. Excited much? Let's get started!

Disclaimer

Please consider using this book for directional purposes and not as an ultimate guide. We made sure that all the contents in the book are as accurate as possible. However, there might be some minor errors in content or typography. Hence, use this guide with the utmost care and double-check the facts before making an actual investment.

This guide is designed by professional authors who have years of experience in their respective fields. They might have got this information from various sources or their own experience. That doesn't mean their predictions can't go wrong. Also, this guide links to various investments and related financial products that the authors have used before.

The ideas/suggestions provided by the authors in this book are simply the ones that have worked for them before. They make no claims that these suggestions will work no matter what. So please be careful before making any real investments and verify the actualities before making decisions. Always remember that due diligence is crucial while making investments in crypto space.

Both the author and the published hold no responsibility for the funds you are going to invest and the losses that you may incur. The whole purpose of this guide is to educate and direct you on the right path while making investment decisions. The author and the publisher shall hold no responsibility or liability to any individual or entity concerning any damage or loss caused or alleged to be caused directly or indirectly by this e-book.

Copyright © 2020 Juan Xie All Rights Reserved

No part of this book may be reproduced, or stored in a retrieval system, or transmitted in any form or by any means, electronic, mechanical, photocopying, recording, or otherwise, without express written permission of the author.

Table of Contents

Session 1 - Introduction to Crypto currency — 9
- What is Crypto currency? — 10
- Brief History — 10
- Current Scenario — 10

Session 2 - Bitcoin - The First Ever Crypto currency — 12
- Origin — 12
- Properties of Bitcoin — 13
- Price History — 14

Session 3 - Blockchain Technology — 16
- What is Blockchain? — 16
- Working of Blockchain — 16
- Smart Contracts — 17

Session 4 - Comprehending Alt-Coins — 18
- The Birth of Altcoins — 18
- Altcoins Types — 18
- Their Relationship with Bitcoin — 19
- The Purpose — 20

Session 5 - Bitcoins vs. Banks — 21
- How does Bitcoin Work? — 21
- Bitcoin - A Threat to Traditional Banks? — 22
- The After Effects! — 22
- Advantages of Bitcoin Over the Traditional Banking System — 23

Session 6 - How To Invest In Cryptos? — 24
- Cryptocurrency and Investing - The Basics — 24
- Getting Started — 24
- Storing Your Cryptos — 25
- 'Investing' in Bitcoin - The Right Term? — 26

Session 7 - Top 5 High Potential Cryptos to Look Out For — 27
- Market Capitalization — 27
- Liquidity — 27
- Top 5 Cryptos to look out for — 27
- Consider these two cryptos as well — 31
- Other unpopular yet high potential crypto currencies — 33

Session 8 - Fundamental & Technical Analysis — 34
- FA & TA of Top 5 Cryptos — 34

Session 9 - Risk Management Techniques You Must Know! — 42
- Why is Risk Management crucial? — 42
- Risk Management Techniques — 42

Introduction to Cryptocurrency

What is a Cryptocurrency?

The term Crypto is derived from a Greek word 'Kruptos' which essentially means something that is hidden or a secret. We are aware of the term currency which implies the money that is currently being used as a medium of exchange. The term crypto is also taken from the technology known as cryptography. This tech enables the smooth functioning of cryptos while hiding identities, information and increasing the security of a transaction.

In simple terms, a cryptocurrency is the cash that is completely virtual and exist in electronic devices in the form of a code. The purpose of cryptos is to form an alternative currency system that is completely decentralized. That is, there won't be any centralized authority like banks or financial institutions monitoring the transactions that we make using cryptos.

The transactions that we make using cryptos are way too faster compared to the traditional wire transfers. The transacting costs involved are much lesser relative to the conventional means. More than anything else, the cryptos are reliable than the fiat currencies that are issued by our governments. The ideology behind the formation of cryptos is this - To create our own money and give it some intrinsic value than to trust the governments and banks to store our hard earned cash.

You storing and transacting cryptocurrency is more or less being your own bank. Because there is no centralized authority here who is monitoring all the transactions that you are performing. Ideally, while transacting cryptos, banks do the job of verifying and validating the transactions. Since it is a decentralized environment, individuals who are transacting cryptos get to verify not just their own transactions but everyone else's transactions as well.

When you are sending a crypto to someone, you are essentially broadcasting a message to the network. This message consist of all the details related to the transaction like who you are, who are you sending it to, and the amount of crypto that is being transferred. All of these transaction details will be recorded in a public ledger that is available for everyone in the network. Hence all the transactions that happen in the network are transparent. This ledger cannot be tampered no matter what hence increasing the security. We will be discussing more about this ledger and the ground breaking technology behind it in the upcoming sessions.

Brief History

The electronic virtual currencies have originated way before the inception of the first ever scalable crypto - Bitcoin. However, these currencies weren't termed cryptos because they do not have the cryptography tech embedded in them. But these are the very first attempts which have eventually lead to the invention of the cryptocurrencies that are currently being used.

The revolution of digital currencies started in the Netherlands way back in 1980s. To avoid the thefts in the Gas Stations that are happening at nights, a group of developers invented an electronic card system. Whoever wants to access Gas can use those cards and hence the use of real money is eliminated.

The second attempt towards virtual currencies is taken by 'David Chaum.' He is an American cryptographer and the inventor of Blinded Cash. The USP of this currency is that it is untraceable. That is, transactions made using this virtual currency cannot be traced. Chaum used complex encryption techniques to achieve this feat. However, this crypto has remained a failed attempt because of various scalability issues.

B Money, Bit Gold are Hash Cash are some of the notable failed attempts in this space that we must know. B Money was portrayed as an electronic cash system that is anonymous and secured at the same time. Bit Gold is considered the first digital asset with a complete decentralized functionality. It is pegged to the value of gold while moving away from centralization.

HashCash got all the things in place except for scalability. It functions almost like Bitcoin and has similar consensus algorithm too. This digital currency was truly ahead of its time and that could be one of the reasons for its failure. Finally in 2008, the whitepaper of Bitcoin is released while in early 2009, the first ever Bitcoin block is mined and the rest is history.

The Current Scenario

Bitcoin's huge success has paved the way for numerous crypto concepts. As of today (May 2020), there are more than 5,500 cryptocurrencies in the market. The total market capitalization of crypto industry is about $250 billion. The 24-hour transactional volume is close to $98 billion dollars. It is no surprise that Bitcoin dominates about 65.5% of the total crypto market. For more information on the same, you can visit coinmarketcap.com.

Various global companies such as Microsoft are accepting Bitcoin as a mode of payment for the services they provide. Companies like Facebook are coming up with their own cryptocurrency (Libra) to overcome some of the challenges faced by cryptos that we are using today. Also, more importantly, even national governments like Federal Reserve have partnered with cryptos like Ripple to increase the efficiency of their cross border payments.

Hence we can say that the acceptance of cryptos is increasing with time and the impact of them in our daily lives is inevitable.

Bitcoin - The First Ever Cryptocurrency

Origin

In 2008, the financial crisis was going on in full throttle. As a matter of fact, Lehman Brother Holdings, fourth largest bank back then, filed for Chapter 11 bankruptcy. During this time, when the financial markets crippled, a domain named Bitcoin.org came into existence on the internet. Following this, a person or group named Satoshi Nakamoto published a white paper relating to Bitcoin that explained the need and working of cryptocurrency.

At the beginning of the very next year, the first-ever cryptocurrency was mined by pseudonym Satoshi Nakamoto. Later, the first Bitcoin transaction took place as well, when Nakamoto sent a Bitcoin to Hal Finney, a cryptograph professional and enthusiast.

In was in 2010, when a programmer from Florida named Lazlo Hanyecz made an offer to purchase a couple of pizzas in exchange for 10,000 Bitcoins. The offer was accepted by a British enthusiast where he ordered the pizzas to be delivered at Hanyecz's residence by paying via credit card. Then, Hanyecz claimed the purchase with 10,000 Bitcoins. This is believed to be the first-ever transaction through Bitcoin. In fact, the Bitcoin community celebrates May 22 as Bitcoin Pizza Day.

Bitcoin in big hands

In the first quarter of 2013, the circulation value of Bitcoin hit an all-time high of $1 billion. This milestone was arbitrary to account for, but soon after, Bitcoin got attracted by big players and venture capitalists. And Winklevoss twins were one of the well-known early investors. The capital they invested came from collecting a $65 million settlement from Mark Zuckerberg. Later, they went on to become the majority owners in another virtual currency called Gemini, after they realized the challenges in buying and selling Bitcoins.

Finally, when Bitcoin began to skyrocket in late 2017, it got extremely popular among the people. Even non-investors started to research and invest in Bitcoin. On a side note, Blockchain, the technology behind Bitcoin, got high recognition as well. In the present day, blockchain technology is evolving to be the next revolutionary technology. But Bitcoin could not sustain at the $20,000 mark and lost about 80% its value the following year. Having said that, Bitcoin is still one of the most traded cryptocurrencies in the world.

Properties of Bitcoin

A hype for Bitcoin was created when the prices shot up like an exponential function. It was considered to be the money of the future. And the reasons for these beliefs come from the properties of the Bitcoin cryptocurrency. When compared to fiat currencies, Bitcoin has astonishing properties and features that cannot be found in fiat currencies. Even when compared to other digital currencies, Bitcoin still stands out through its properties. The following are some significant properties of Bitcoin that are not embedded in other types of currencies.

Decentralized

The decentralization of Bitcoin was one of the primary objectives of Satoshi Nakamoto. He wished to design a payment system that did not involve any government authority during the course of the transaction. There is no intermediary like the banks to validate the transaction in a Bitcoin transaction between the sender and receiver. Instead, it is a network of distributed peers across the world.

Anonymity

When a transaction is made through a bank, the bank basically knows everything about the client, which could include credit history, phone number, ID, address, etc. With Bitcoin, all transactions are essentially anonymous, as a Bitcoin wallet provider does not require their clients to provide personal identifying information. Moreover, all the transaction history is open in public but cannot be tracked by any kind of authority.

Security

The transactions on Bitcoin are highly secure as the system uses cryptographic techniques to safeguard Bitcoins. In addition, blockchain technology uses the consensus algorithm that makes Bitcoin transactions immutable and hence puts another layer of security.

Irreversible and non-alterable

Once a transaction is confirmed on the Bitcoin blockchain, there is no way it can be reversed. This is because the transaction is stored in a chain of blocks. To alter or tamper with a transaction, a hacker will have to figure out all the blocks involved in the transaction, which is practically impossible.

Instant Payments

Bitcoin works on the blockchain network, which is essentially a distributed ledger. The transactions are headed over the network and are confirmed within minutes of time. Since it is a global network, there are no barriers over international transactions, unlike the banking system. Thus, the location of the sender and the receiver is insignificant in Bitcoin transactions.

Price History

The below chart explains how the value of Bitcoin has changed with time.

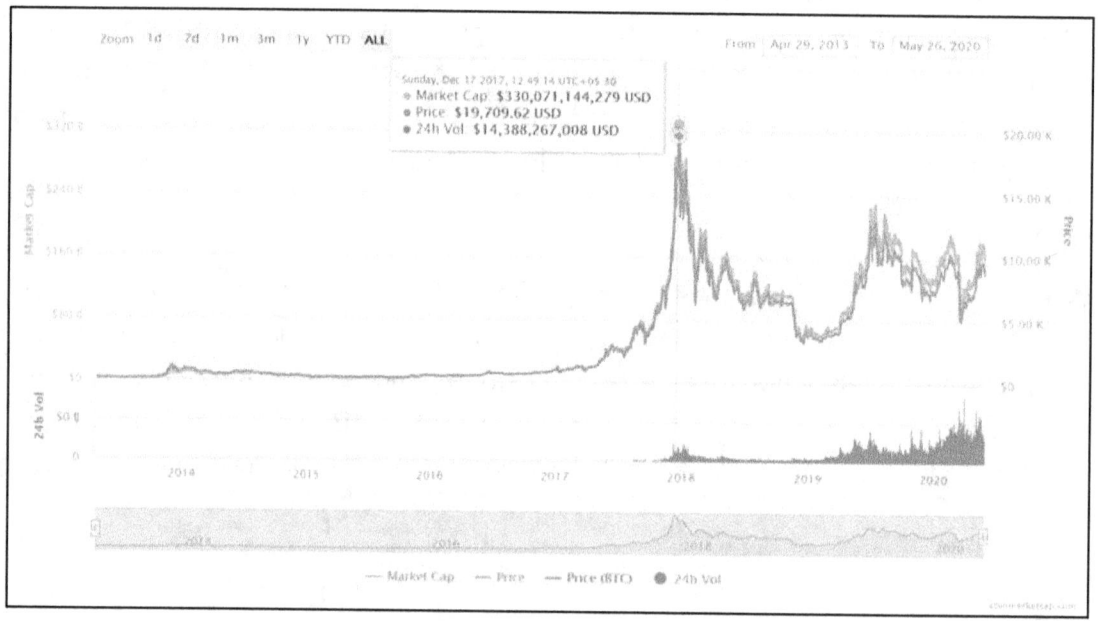

(Chart Credits - coinmarketcap.com)

Bitcoin started to possess real value in the end of 2012 which is after four years of its first transaction. It was somewhere closer to $14 at that time. The first swing high has occurred in the first half of 2013 where the price crossed $200 mark. Gradually the price started to fluctuate throughout the year and in November 2013, Bitcoin's value crossed the $1000 mark. Ever since then, the price was hovering around this value till the mid of 2017.

That year, the price of this crypto has crossed the $5000 mark and doubled in less than a month to cross the $10,000 mark. Finally, in December 2017, Bitcoin achieved its ATH (All Time High) value and this grabbed the attention of the people across the world. Currently, the value of Bitcoin is close to $9000 and is expected to increase very soon.

According to a lot of crypto expert opinions, the reason for the increase in Bitcoin's value is because of one concept called Bitcoin Halving. To understand this we must know what a block reward means. For every successful block mined, a miner will get a certain number of coins as reward. We know that, in the Bitcoin network, a block is mined every 10 minutes. So every 10 minutes few Bitcoins are released in the market, thereby increasing it supply.

These rewards are reduced to half after certain number of blocks are added to the blockchain. This process is known as halving. It is crucial to reduce the supply to increase the demand of the coin in order to increase its value. So at this rate, the rewards will be stopped at one point and the supply ends there. For Bitcoin, the total supply ends when a total of 21 Million coins are mined. It is forecasted that the last ever Bitcoin may be mined in the year 2140.

The initial block reward used to 50 Bitcoins for every block mined until the first halving happened in 2012. Since then, the reward got reduced to 25 coins until the second halving occurred in 2016, reducing the block reward to 12.5 coins. The third halving occurred in May 2020 and currently the block reward is reduced to 6.25 Bitcoins per block mined.

If you can see the above graph, it is clear that the Bitcoin's value took off from literally nothing to ~$14 right after the first halving. Then, the 2016 halving has enabled Bitcoin to achieve its ATH value. That is the reason why we said the value will increase very soon as Bitcoin completed its third halving. The reason for the value to increase after halving is due to the decrease in supply. As the supply decreases, the demand of the Bitcoin increases and thereby its value.

Blockchain Technology

What is a Blockchain?

Blockchain is often confused to the first ever cryptocurrency - Bitcoin. This is because the term blockchain became popular only after the inception of Bitcoin. In reality, blockchain is the primary technology that enables the working of cryptos. If not for blockchain, we won't be seeing any of the cryptocurrencies that are in circulation today. It is important to know that cryptocurrency is just one of the various potential applications of blockchain technology.

In simple terms, blockchain is a distributed electronic ledger that is built around a Peer 2 Peer system. This ledger can be shared among infinite number of users for their individual reference. The transactions that are entered in the blockchain are tamper proof and are time-stamped individually. A set of valid transactions makes a block complete. Each of the verified blocks is linked to the previous block to form a chain of blocks. Hence the name - Blockchain!

Working of Blockchain

The working of the Blockchain is different from that of centralized systems. It is a distributed ledger and works as a network on the basis of consensus, thus, making it decentralized. Following is the step by step working of a transaction on the Blockchain.

1. A node, which is basically a computer in the blockchain network, receives a transaction from the sender. It initiates that transaction on the network by creating it. Later, it gets the transaction digitally signed with a private key using the cryptography technique.

2. The transaction information is passed from that node to all the other nodes on the network to validate the transaction based on some criteria preset by the Blockchain. This process is called the Gossip protocol. In technical terms, it is called the Proof of Work, which is the standard consensus algorithm of Blockchain. According to the algorithm, the nodes must solve a complex mathematical puzzle to authenticate a transaction. Usually, two or more nodes are required to validate the transaction.

3. Once the nodes completely validate the transaction, it is included inside a block and is propagated towards the main blockchain network. This is when the **transaction gets its first confirmation.**

4. Later, when a new block is created for the same transaction, it goes through the same process above and gets linked to the first block, referred to as the **"genesis block."** Now, the **block gets its first confirmation**, and the **transaction gets its second confirmation.**

5. For every new block created, the same process continues and is reconfirmed repeatedly. Typically, about five-six confirmations are required for the transaction to be officially complete. And finally, the ownership of the cryptocurrency/digital asset is moved to the receiver.

Smart Contracts

One of the most fundamental purposes of using a blockchain is that there are no middle man involved. Because, blockchain is decentralized and all the functions that are done by the middle men are replaced with complex computer algorithms. A revolutionary application of blockchain that has the potential to eliminate a lot of intermediaries is known as Smart Contracts.

Smart Contracts can be defined as a computerized agreement that can be stored in a blockchain network. In smart contracts, all the terms of a contract can be pre-coded and the execution of these contracts can automatically be done once the conditions of the contract are met. Since these Smart Contracts are stored in a blockchain network, the security, transparency and accessibility of the contract is increased exponentially.

Also, these smart-contracts are immutable. That is, they are tamper proof and it is impossible for anyone to change the terms once the contract is activated. If any of the involved parties makes an attempt to alter the contract terms, the contract will get rejected while intimating all the involved parties. More importantly, these contracts are cost effective as we can eliminate the fees we pay to typical intermediaries such as authorizers, document creators etc.

Comprehending Alt-Coins

The Birth of Altcoins

In 2009, Bitcoin, the first cryptocurrency, was launched. Back then, it barely had any popularity. But, within few years, as people started to understand the working and benefits of Bitcoin and the technology behind it, they also realized the downsides in them. And thus, came other cryptocurrencies to address the issues in Bitcoin.

Altcoins are the cryptocurrencies launched after Bitcoin. The term altcoin is derived from two words 'alt' and 'coins,' which means **alt**ernatives to Bitcoin. They consist of all the coins apart from Bitcoin. In early 2020, there were over 5,000 altcoins in the market. As per CoinMarketCap, 34 percent of the total cryptocurrency market is made of altcoins.

Most of the altcoins are designed on the framework of Bitcoin. That is, they are peer-to-peer. They aim to present an efficient and inexpensive way to make transactions over the internet across the world. Though there are a lot of them, they do vary in their features.

Altcoins Types

The evolution of altcoins led to the classification of them. Out of the many, here are some main types of Bitcoin.

Mining-based

These are the coins that are created through mining by solving complex mathematical problems. They are very similar to Bitcoin. Ethereum is one of the best-known examples in this category.

Stable Coin

These are the cryptocurrencies created to improve Bitcoin by reducing its volatility. This is achieved by attaching the value of the coins with traditional currencies. Some of the popular choices for backing these coins include the US dollar, the euro, and even gold for that matter. Facebook's Libra is considered to be a stable coin. However, it is not launched yet.

Security Tokens

Security tokens are altcoins that are linked to a business. They are launched in an Initial Coin Offering (ICO), just like Initial Public Offering (IPO) in stocks They, in fact, have some features of stocks, where some of the coins pay dividends to their investors.

Utility Tokens

These are the tokens that provide a right on services and can be sold in an ICO. Filecoin is a popular utility coin offered in an ICO. Filecoins were created with an aim to be exchangeable for file storage space, which is decentralized.

Their Relationship with Bitcoin

It is a known fact that Bitcoin is a cryptocurrency. But it can be comprehended as software that runs by the people called Bitcoin Core, which is backed by the blockchain technology, which keeps a track on who has which Bitcoins. However, Bitcoin has no domination on blockchain technology. Anyone can create their own cryptocurrency and blockchain for it, which is the typical meaning of cryptocurrencies.

Initially, when altcoins came into the market, many were unaware of it. This is because people were highly inclined towards Bitcoin. But, when they began to understand the shortcomings in Bitcoin, they turned to altcoins. As a result, they gained immense popularity. Here are some of those coins.

Ether

Ether is one of the most popular altcoins that is generated on the Ethereum network. Sometimes this cryptocurrency is also referred to as Ethereum. The Ethereum platform is an open-source ledger technology used for building decentralized applications. CryptoKitties is an online game, is a popular smart contract that runs on the Ethereum network. In fact, it accounts for 11 percent of all the transactions on the network.

Ripple

Ripple is another alternative for Bitcoin, owned by a private company. As a matter of fact, the name of the company is Ripple, and its tokens are also referred to by the same name. Its ticker is XRP. Ripple has grown to the extent that; it is used by some banks to settle cross-border payments. However, technically, they are sending digital IOUs and finally settling with traditional currencies rather than using them as XRP coins.

Bitcoin Cash

Initially, Bitcoin cash was the fork of Bitcoin. But later, it went on to become a separate cryptocurrency. It is basically an up-gradation to Bitcoin, with architectural changes, leading to the faster transaction along with lower fees relative to Bitcoin.

Litecoin

Similar to Bitcoin Cash, Litecoin was also a fork of Bitcoin when it was launched. This token uses a different Proof-of-Work algorithm that is more memory intensive. Whereas Bitcoin's algorithm is more processing power intensive. The Litecoin network tries to confirm blocks four times faster than the Bitcoin network, thus increasing transaction confirmation speed.

Monero

Monero is just another cryptocurrency created with an aim to be "secure, private, and untraceable." It is quite different from that of Bitcoin blockchain, transactions on the Monero blockchain cannot be tracked back to individual users. Therefore, it makes it popular in the domain of online drugs.

The Purpose

We know that Bitcoin is the first cryptocurrency that came into the market. Being a unique digital currency, it has its own predefined rules. And the reason for the creation of altcoins lies in these rules. Some of the rules and facts include

- It takes 10 minutes on the network to create a new coin.
- It requires a lot of computing power to mine Bitcoins.
- The maximum number of Bitcoins that can be mined is 21 million.
- Bitcoin was created to be a form of digital money and nothing more.

These were the significant choices that were made when the creators of Bitcoin designed their protocol. And there is a restriction for the rules to change. However, the team that manages the software side of Bitcoin is conservative and is not keen on making changes to it, or the rules in them. And the reasons for it are on the positive side. Bitcoin, presently, has a market cap of billions of dollars, and many firms rely on it. So, bringing changes to the current technology could create problems for those who depend highly on this cryptocurrency. Thus, to address and come up with a solution to the above rules and facts, altcoins were created.

Bitcoin vs. Banks

Bitcoin was created with an aim to decentralize the financial system. In other terms, it was designed to replace the centralized banking system. To date, it has not officially been able to capture the banks, but the efforts are still intact. So, the dominance of Bitcoin over banks would decentralize the banking system. Thus, we need to concentrate on the characteristics and features of decentralized systems and centralized systems to understand if Bitcoin is really capable of taking over the current banking system.

How does Bitcoin Work?

Before the introduction to Bitcoin in the market, we were exposed only to the working of the traditional banking system. Bitcoin and other cryptocurrencies work by storing the transactions on a decentralized public ledger. The ledger uses cryptographic algorithms to ensure that records in them are on point and the user's identity is encrypted.

Bitcoin owners have digital wallets where they can store their coins. And the work of the ledger is to ensure that accurate spendable balance is maintained in the wallet. Moreover, it tracks the transaction history to ensure that the owner is spending from their own wallets.

Bitcoin, unlike traditional currencies, is not created through the printing of notes and coins. But are created through a process called 'cryptocurrency mining.' Mining is the process of solving complex mathematical puzzles to confirm a transaction and add it to the ledger (block). Now that you know the basic working, we can go ahead and understand its implications on banks.

Implications for Banks

In recent years, there has been a drastic change in how people look at businesses and make transactions. Presently, one can exchange currency outside of traditional banks with a few clicks on a mobile phone.

A significant point here is that people need not physically go to a traditional bank if they require financing. With the development of the peer-to-peer network, as in the case of Bitcoin and other cryptocurrencies, are getting much popular and common, and people are turning away for banks and looking forward to more decentralized systems like Bitcoin.

Bitcoin - A Threat to Traditional Banks?

In short, perhaps, yes. Cryptocurrency enthusiasts have long ago identified that Bitcoin and its technology is a threat to the banking industry. Not just them, but banks too have strong perceptions on the replacement of working of banks with the blockchain technology. For instance, BNP Paribas, a French banking giant, released a report regarding their discussion on the technology behind Bitcoin and the possibilities on how it could make traditional banks redundant.

Furthermore, an analyst for the bank compared the software behind Bitcoin with an invention like steam and combustion engine and stated that it has the potential to transform the world of finance. A UK banking report concluded that Bitcoin and the following cryptocurrencies definitely are a menace to traditional banks, especially if they do not consider the new preferences and behaviors of people on how they wish to transact with money.

The After Effects!

To understand Bitcoin's power, let us assume a scenario where Bitcoin has taken over the financial system. Here are effects banks can have with the entry of Bitcoin in the world of finance.

- The demise of the banking system

- Banks will not be able to create reserves and perform fractional reserve lending with Bitcoin.

- There is no means through which it can control Bitcoin, as Bitcoin has no representative and is fully decentralized.

- Banks can no longer inflate or deflate away the purchasing power of users' saving accounts.

- Bailouts with Bitcoin cannot be done by banks if cryptocurrencies get adopted worldwide.

- Banks cannot generate revenue from remittance businesses, where they levy 10-30 percent in cross-border transactions.

- Banks act as an intermediary for every transaction that is made. But, with Bitcoin in the market, banks can become inexistent as one of the main features of Bitcoin is the absence of middleman.

These were the list of possibilities that can emerge if Bitcoin comes into the mainstream business. And thus, banks consider Bitcoin as a potential threat to themselves. Moreover, some believe that Bitcoin's impact on banks and the current technology will be beyond one's imagination.

Advantages of Bitcoin Over the Traditional Banking System

Bitcoin, a decentralized system, has several benefits over the centralized system like banks, mainly because of the capability to operate without any intermediary and no case of failure at any point.

Processing of Transactions

Local transactions in the banking system are settled quickly. However, when it comes to international fund transfers, banks take several days to process the transaction. Bitcoin, a peer-to-peer payment system, on the other hand, can process over $1 billion worth of transactions on an average. Thus, irrespective of the sender and receiver location, transactions are processed within a few minutes. Banks work for five business days, and typically no transactions are settled during the weekend or holidays. Meanwhile, Bitcoin is open every single day and has no concept of holidays and weekends.

Offshore Banking

Financial institutions like JP Morgan, who dominate the offshore banking industry, have links with large banks that make it possible to clear billions of money very efficiently and securely. However, a downside is that the transfer of billions of dollars requires considerable manual labor that includes verification of the transaction, Anti-money Laundering checks, and payment clearing. But, Bitcoin, being completely decentralized, does not require any sort of manual labor, as mentioned. Moreover, settlement and offshore banking are provided by Bitcoin with significantly lesser costs and much robust infrastructure.

In conclusion, everything boils down to one question: Can Bitcoin take over the Banking system? Yes and no. With the incredible benefits Bitcoin offers, there is a possibility of Bitcoin ruling over the banking system. Having that said, since the traditional banking system is a mature structure, people rely upon and believe in this system. At the same time, Bitcoin does have downsides in terms of volatility and regulation. Therefore, it cannot be said with certainty that Bitcoin will replace the existing centralized system, even though it capable of doing so.

How to Invest In Cryptos?

The cryptocurrency market has been in the market relatively shorter than other traditional markets. However, it has expanded widely. This is sole because of the features cryptocurrencies have to offer. Bitcoin and every other cryptocurrency are known for its high volatility, giving massive gain opportunities for investors if they can digest the risk.

Cryptocurrency is an online market, and there are several digital platforms that have simplified it, people, to invest in this market. However, comparatively, it is much complicated than acquiring traditional currencies. If you're new to this domain and willing to invest cryptos, here's everything you need to know.

Cryptocurrency and Investing - The Basics

There are thousands of cryptocurrencies present market, and figuring out where to put your money becomes intimidating. Looking from a broader perspective, every cryptocurrency is highly encrypted, and most of them are decentralized as well. But Bitcoin is the first cryptocurrency and most recognized in the market that runs on the blockchain technology. Hence, this makes Bitcoin one of the most reliable coins out there.

Many investors are inclined towards investing in only Bitcoin and a few other popular currencies. For instance, people are keen on investing in Ethereum, where they attempt to buy low and sell high in belief that it can be the next Bitcoin.

Any cryptocurrency you invest in, there is a common denominator – volatility. A fact with cryptocurrencies is that they have value as long as people comprehend it to have value. Though it is technically true with any kind of currency, it is more significant with cryptos as they are not backed by the government or precious metals, like other traditional currencies. Therefore, investing in cryptos comes with added risks.

Getting Started

Investing in cryptocurrency basically means buying them and keeping them stored. So, to invest in cryptocurrency, we need to research on where to buy and store the coins. Cryptocurrency exchanges are the places cryptocurrency can be purchased. They are online platforms that allow exchanging coins with fiat currencies or other digital assets.

There several cryptocurrency exchanges out there on the internet. It is necessary to choose the right one as it is where you will buy, sell, exchange, and store the digital assets. Some of the most popular crypto exchanges include Coinbase, GDAx, and Bitfinex. Apart from being popular, they are the most reliable exchanges available. These are the exchanges where you can buy cryptocurrencies like Bitcoin and Ethereum using your bank account or a debit card. However, these are fiat to crypto exchanges, which allows the buying and selling of cryptos using only fiat currencies. In other words, you cannot buy a cryptocurrency with the help of another cryptocurrency.

So, you will have to approach another cryptocurrency exchange that allows trading of cryptocurrency with others. One such example of the same is **Binance**. This exchange facilitates traders to buy and sell cryptocurrencies for other cryptocurrencies. In a technical sense, you can trade pairs like ETH/BTC and XRP/BTC, rather than just BTC/USD or ETH/USD. Thus, you need not involve traditional currencies in the business.

Besides these two types of exchanges, there is another type which allows participants to buy and sell their cryptocurrencies directly. LocalBitcoins is one of the oldest and most popular portals for direct one-to-one transactions of cryptocurrencies. The prices here are set by the sellers themselves, not the exchange. However, this is the least preferred route to buy and invest cryptocurrencies as involves direct transaction with a stranger whose currency cannot be verified as such. So, if you're new to cryptocurrency investing, it is recommended to start off with an exchange like Coinbase.

Another infamous option that's recently getting more prevalent is Bitcoin ATM. As per sources, there are over 4,000 cryptocurrencies ATM locations in seventy-six countries presently. These can be used to purchase Bitcoin and send it over to your cryptocurrency wallet.

Storing Your Cryptos

The term 'cryptocurrency wallet' is often used when it comes to storing coins. And that is because cryptocurrency wallet is a device or software that allows users to store and retrieve their digital assets. And this wallet represents your portfolio. For instance, when you create an account with Coinbase, you automatically get a software wallet for yourself. If you purchase any cryptocurrency, it will be reflected in your Coinbase wallet. This amount can further be used to send it to other exchanges for crypto-to-crypto trading.

'Investing' in Bitcoin - The Right Term?

From the launch of Bitcoin to date, we have observed a bell curve movement in prices. That is, initially, it started off slow, skyrocketed to $20,000 in 2017, couldn't sustain, and dropped to levels around $3500. And this represents the volatility of Bitcoin.

So, investing in cryptocurrency is quite different from that of traditional investments. However, the risk analysis can be performed the same way. Like any other investment, you must clearly weigh your potential profits against the risk you're are willing to take. Investing in cryptocurrency comes from the type of trader you are. If you are a conservative investor looking to minimize risk and grow profits over time, then cryptocurrency might not be the right choice for investment. Conversely, if you can bear the high risk to considerably maximize your profits, then you could try your hand in this market.

Bitcoin and altcoins are markets with inconsistent growth and significant volatility. Thus, the term 'speculation' goes accurately with the above description than the term 'investing.'

Top 5 High Potential Cryptos to Look Out For

Cryptocurrencies had seen a significant devaluation in 2020. However, there still are coins that have a high potential to yield good returns to investors. Cryptocurrencies don't function like any other market where the current rate matters in analyzing the security. Cryptocurrencies are highly volatile, and their prices may change drastically within a matter of weeks or so. Instead, the following are the factors that must be considered:

Market Capitalization

It is the **value** of all the issued coins of a particular cryptocurrency. A large market capitalization of a coin means that the participating volume is high, and there are numerous active transactions, implying the interest of investors.

Liquidity

It is the ease with which a trader can buy or sell a cryptocurrency at the market price. In a highly liquid market, one can get filled very close to the market price. It is an indicator of the demand in a cryptocurrency in traders.

Based on these two factors and several others, here are the top five cryptocurrencies that have a brighter future ahead.

1. Bitcoin

Bitcoin was the first-ever crypto ever created. Even after its ups and downs over a decade, it has still managed to be the most popular cryptocurrency. It is the first digital currency that features completely decentralized and secure transactions, which is indeed the heart of Bitcoin. The potential of cryptos as a whole is huge. But Bitcoin is the one that has successfully made into the real-world market as well.

Some several online portals and retailers allow Bitcoin as a payment option, showing people are using it as a part of their everyday life. It is not as widely accepted as PayPal or Neteller, but there are positive indications that show a gradual yet significant increase in Bitcoin as a tool of payment. Thus, keeping the demand for Bitcoin up and going.

As per sources, Bitcoin developers will offer 50 percent reduced rewards to miners for verification of blocks. Moreover, there are high possibilities of Bitcoin bringing the dominance level to 65 to 70 percent compared to other coins. Thus, it can continue to maintain as a cryptocurrency with the largest market capitalization. In addition, the use of Lightning Network could perhaps change the ecosystem of Bitcoin. Thus, all these factors can prove to be a potential coin to look out for.

2. Ethereum

After Bitcoin, Ethereum is next on our list. Ethereum runs on the second-generation blockchain, an upgraded version of the first-generation blockchain technology used in Bitcoin. Ethereum was primarily created to address the limitations of Bitcoin. Bitcoin has inadequate scripting abilities with its peer-to-peer working structure. Without any significant changes, the creator of Ethereum introduced a cryptocurrency having advanced scripting abilities. As a major upgrade, this cryptocurrency came with smart contracts. It is smart contracts that sustain Ethereum from its launch to the present date.

Ethereum is based on a decentralized platform that enables users to interact with smart contracts and create Decentralized Applications (DApps) without any downtime or control from a third party. These apps are highly secure and free from outside attacks as they are not centralized. These applications are fueled by Ethereum's own cryptographic token, Ether.

This altcoin was launched in 2015 and is presently the second-largest cryptocurrency in terms of market capitalization after Bitcoin. That being said, it still significantly lags from Bitcoin, as its market cap is no more than one-tenth of the most dominant cryptocurrency. Nonetheless, there is a firm belief in this cryptocurrency technology for the product it offers.

Ethereum can become the core technology in Bank loans, insurance claims, mortgages, and many other financial sectors in the coming years. Thus, leading to an increase in demand going further.

3. Ripple

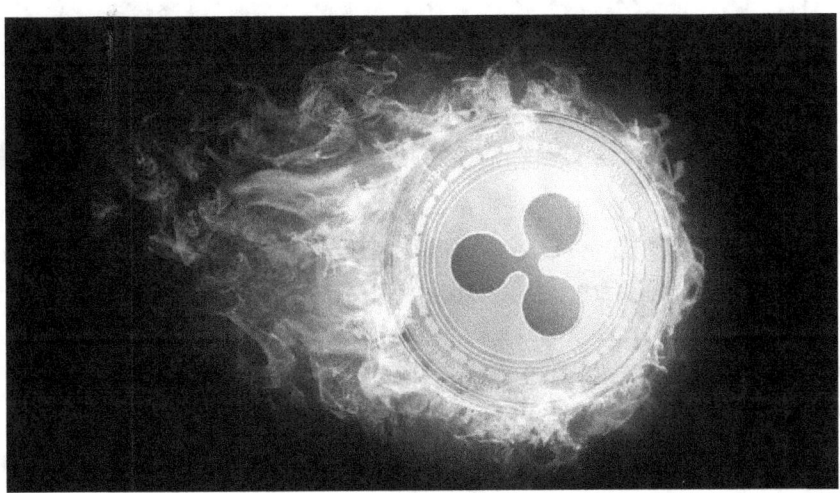

Ripple was a technology built to enable banks with the ability to exchange money via a decentralized network. Although it seems to be similar to Ethereum, it neither completely decentralized nor it uses smart contracts for transactions. Ripple stands out from Bitcoin and Ethereum transaction processing speed.

It can process up to 1,500 transactions per second. This platform, too, has a token XRP that can be used to over the network for exchanging money. These coins are significantly different from BTC as they are already mined.

Big banks and payment services can take full advantage of Ripple technology and revolutionize the existing system. If a bank or payment provider implements the Ripple technology into its system, the transaction costs would get considerably cheap and would also offer a transparent mode of payment, unlike the traditional SWIFT payments.

The motive of Bitcoin and Ripple is not the same. Bitcoin was created to use as a form of money, while Ripple was designed to exchange XRP quickly and seamlessly for currencies or commodities. And such technology is the first of its kind. Therefore, in considerations of the features of Ripple, it can turn out to be a gainer in the years to come.

4. Chainlink

Chainlink is an Ethereum built decentralized oracle network. As the name suggests, the network is created to connect off-chain data sources like APIs, feeds, or bank transactions to the on-chain smart contract. It was developed by Sergey Nazarov, who held an ICO in September 2017, raising USD 32m. Chainlink decentralized network has its native cryptocurrency, used as a medium of payment to node operators.

The Chainlink network being a reputed one, node providers with a large number of LINK are usually rewarded with larger contracts. At the same time, the delivery of inaccurate information can lead to a deduction of the reward. Chainlink is a platform that acts as a bridge between smart contracts based on blockchain and real-world applications. Since blockchain does not allow access to data outside their network, a defi instrument called oracles is required as data is fed into smart contracts. In the case of Chainlink, these oracles are connected to the Ethereum network.

5. Tezos

Tezos is a decentralized smart contract and blockchain network that is linked to a digital currency, called Tez. The coin trades under the ticker XTZ. Tezos, unlike Bitcoin, is not based on mining, but the asset holders receive a reward for participating in the Proof-of-Stake consensus mechanism. It was discovered by an ex-Morgan Stanley analyst Arthur Breitman with his wife and launched an ICO in 2017, raising USD 232 million.

Tezos is supported by the Tezos Foundation, a Swiss-based entity that is involved in promoting the Tezos protocol via grants and capital vehicles. Tezos creates incentives for users who wish to participate in the core development of the Tezos protocol. As mentioned, it works on the Proof-of-Stake mechanism, which is powered by Tezos (XTZ) tokens, created through "baking." Baking refers to the way of earning the rewards by staking, where bakers put in deposits and are rewarded for signing and publishing blocks.

Consider these two cryptos as well

Litecoin

Litecoin is a cryptocurrency created two years after the launch of Bitcoin. It was designed following the footsteps of Bitcoin. An ex-Google employee named Charlie Lee invented this coin as an alternative to Bitcoin for making payments. This coin is basically an upgraded version of Bitcoin. The transaction speed in Litecoin is four times as fast as Bitcoin. The total count of Litecoin stands at 84 million LTC, that considerably greater than that of Bitcoin, whose maximum supply is only 21 million BTC.

Litecoin is one of the first altcoins that came into existence. With almost over a decade in the market and its features resembling Bitcoin, it is a highly reliable cryptocurrency. Unlike other altcoins, Litecoin can be bought against traditional currencies like USD, GBP, EUR, and CNY; as a result, it can easily be traded all across the world. Also, the number of merchants accepting Litecoin is growing drastically. As a result, it has bought Litecoin to the sixth position in terms of market cap. Although it is similar to Bitcoin, there still is a demand for this cryptocurrency for the high transaction speed it offers.

Tether

Tether is a popular cryptocurrency that belongs to the stablecoins group. Stablecoins are the coins whose market value is pegged to a currency or a similar referential asset so as to reduce volatility in the pair. It is a known fact that digital currencies, be it Bitcoin or any other cryptocurrency, have dramatic volatility in prices.

Thus, to smooth out drastic price fluctuations, Tether and other stablecoins were created. This would also allow caution or conservative traders to participate in the cryptocurrency market. It was launched in 2014 as RealCoin but got rebranded to Tether in early 2015. This coin has a fixed price that is measured by a fiat currency such as the US dollar. It is abbreviated as USDT.

The maximum supply stands at 4 billion USDT, making it extremely challenging for other stablecoins to compete with. Tether is the most popular and reliable stablecoin, which is extensively used in the investment and trading sectors. Moreover, it is considered to be a safer investment than any other coin with higher volatility. With these factors, Tether became the fourth largest cryptocurrency by market capitalization in early 2020.

Other unpopular yet high potential cryptocurrencies

Currently, there are over 1,000 cryptocurrencies in the crypto market. Their market capitalization and volume are significantly lesser than cryptos like Bitcoin and Ethereum. However, this does not imply that they don't have a bright future ahead. For example, Bitcoin, too, was worth only a few cents but later skyrocketed to $20,000 dollars. Likewise, there are cryptocurrencies that can make a fortune for investors. But, presently, there are so many coins that it is complicated to analyze every cryptocurrency to speculate on it.

Here are few of the coins you should have in your watchlist as they can turn out to be explosive currencies in the years to come:

- ✓ **Zcash**
- ✓ **Basic Attention Token**
- ✓ **Chainlink**
- ✓ **Synthetic Network Token**
- ✓ **DxChain Token**
- ✓ **Tezos**
- ✓ **Zilliqa**

These are coins that have great features and believe they can become the next Bitcoin in the crypto space. However, these coins are meant for the ones who are willing to take the risk to bag big from them. The rest may lookout for those having large market capitalization and enough liquidity.

Fundamental and Technical Analysis

Be it stocks, commodities, or currencies; there are two ways to analyze them – Fundamental and Technical. Cryptocurrencies are no different in this matter. Both Fundamental and Technical analysis can be applied to cryptocurrencies to analyze and predict their future. The technical analysis remains the same as any other market, but the fundamental factors differ.

1. Bitcoin Analysis

Fundamental Analysis

Bitcoin is the first cryptocurrency, and it has been a decade since its launch. There have been several dramatic ups and downs in the prices, but this coin has still sustained well. If were a bubble, it would have collapsed long ago. A ten-year and counting sustainability simply means that people still believe in this cryptocurrency. Thus, keeping the demand still intact and increasing.

In May 2020, the Bitcoin having event took place. And by tradition, it is known to have a positive effect on the market. Bitcoin halving is a reduction in the reward that is paid for mining a successfully. Before May, Bitcoin halving took place twice:

The first halving happened in November 2012, where the price was $12. The price in March 2012, a few months before the event, was at $4, which was three times lesser than the price when it was halved. Similarly, the price in December 2013, a year after the event, the price stood at $994.

The second halving took place in July 2016, when the price of Bitcoin was $650. In January 2016, the price was $431, and the price a year after the event surged to $19,535.

The third and most recent halving took place in May 2020. It is going to be worth noticing the price in the coming year if it will follow the previous trend. However, looking in the supply side of things, the halving of Bitcoin will directly impact the new coins coming into the market and will result in slower supply growth. And thus, a drop in supply will inflate the prices of Bitcoin.

Technical Analysis

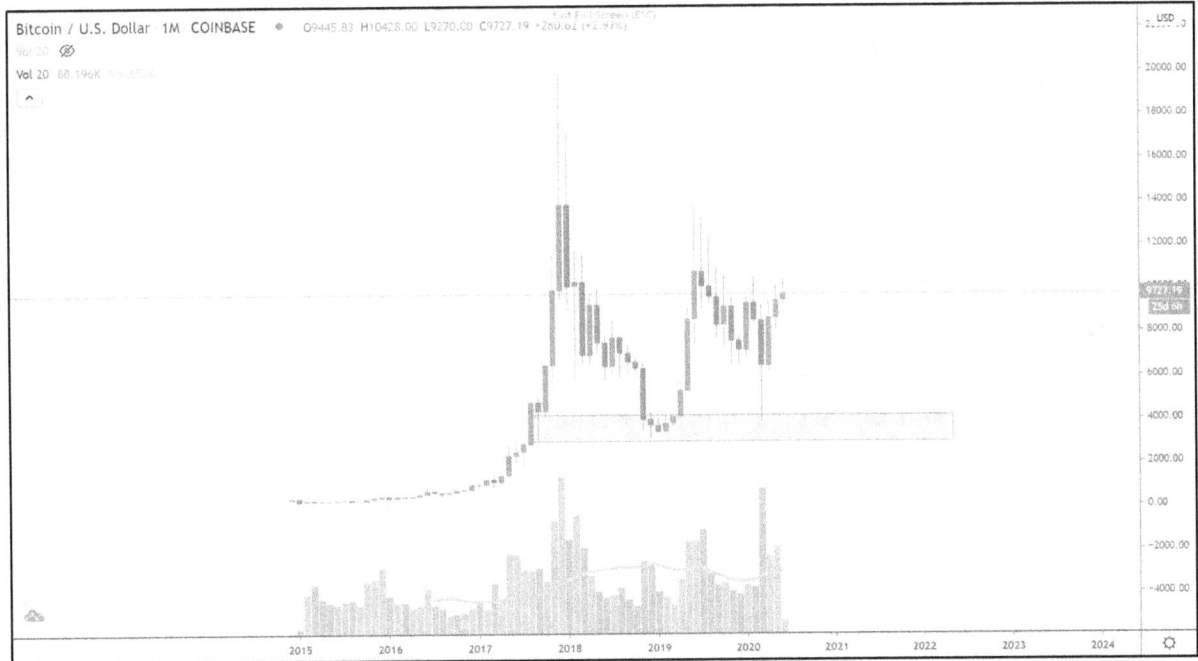

Above is the monthly chart of Bitcoin against the US dollar. Looking at the overall picture, the market is in an uptrend. The massive move to $19,900 began from the area around $3000. With this mind, let's move to a lower time frame to study the fine details in the market.

After making an all-time, the market held at $5900 for almost a year. In the last quarter of 2018, the market broke below the support and came down to the demand region. At levels around $3000 dollars, the price aggressively shot up, respecting the demand zone. Also, note that the market could not push the market down from the support turned resistance level at $5900, indicating the weakness of sellers.

From $12000, the market again came down, but the demand area pushed it right back up. A key point to ascertain here is that the buyers held higher from the previous point, as illustrated by the brown trend line. It even left a wick on the bottom the second time, indicating the buyer's desperation. Thus, we can conclude that the trend is still bullish for Bitcoin. Forecasting for the year, the market could find support at $7500 or $6000 and then go up to levels of $138000 and $17200.

2. Ethereum Analysis

Fundamental Analysis

Fundamental factors such as hash rate, daily active addresses, and transactions per day, have increased over the past few months, in fact, significantly up from the year-end lows it had set in 2019. The ProgPoW consensus algorithm change is most likely to be implemented this year, which will drastically change the mining procedure of Ethereum. There have always been updated in the Ethereum network, and the coming upgrade is a significant one, called 'Ethereum 2.0.' It has not launched yet, but there are active talks and discussions on the release of phase zero of ETH 2.0. Thus, the fundamentals of Ethereum are strong and could get stronger in the coming months.

Technical Analysis

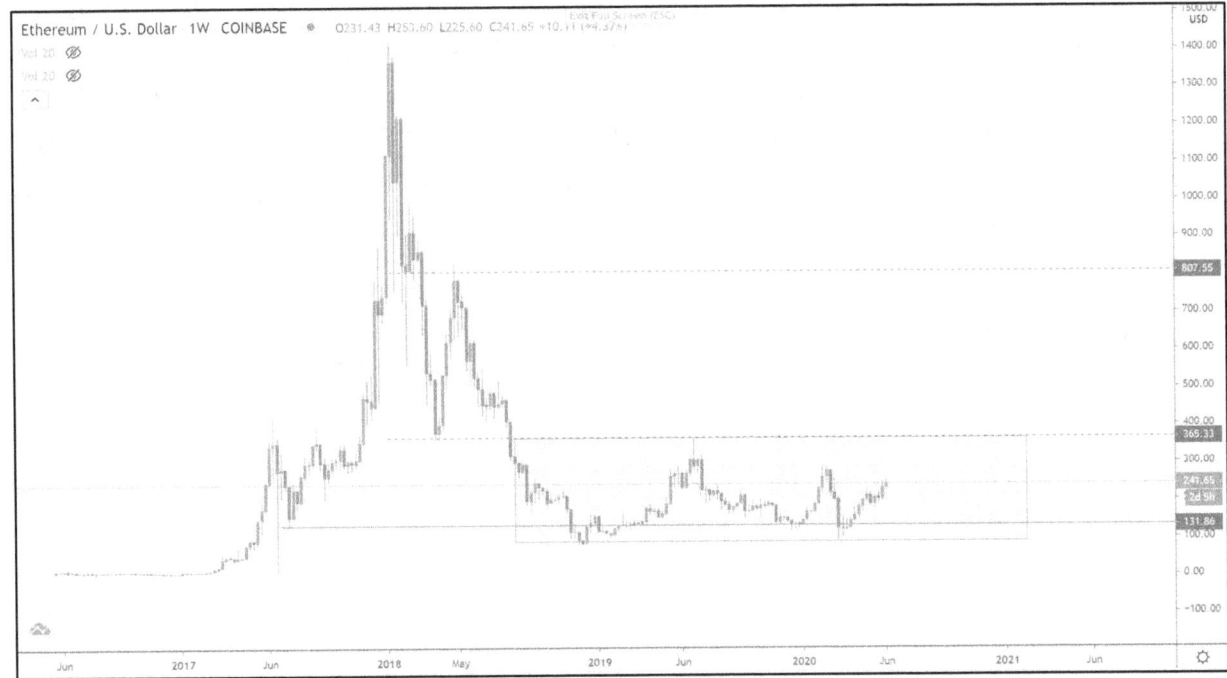

Below is the chart of Ethereum on the weekly time frame. When compared, it is similar to that of Bitcoin. From $100, the price went up all the way to $1400. It failed to make a higher high and come rolling down. It found support at $365 but broke below it as well. Finally, it came to the demand zone around $131 and began to range between this level and $365. Thus, we find that Ethereum is currently in a range. In the short term, there are possibilities of Ethereum touching the $400 mark. In the long term, given the fundamentals still stay firm, this market can break above the range and trend up to $800, which is about 225% from current levels.

3. Ripple Analysis

Fundamental Analysis

The fundamental analysis of Ripple can be broken down into two major catalysts. The first type is called the 'traction' as per the 'Lean Startup' principles. And the second is the massive capital inflow coming from Wall Street, said by institutional investors.

There are clear signs of traction in Ripple, which is the most critical piece in our fundamental analysis. Ripple has a vast network enabling cross-border payments. It has a decentralized network of financial institutions referred to as RippleNet that allows sending and settling payments internationally on-demand. RippleNet is a fast, inexpensive, and transparent payment service, which is now active over 40 countries across six continents. Moreover, Ripple has a wide range of products such as xVia, xCurrent, and xRapid that work seamlessly, and increase the usage of the XRP token.

Technical Analysis

Above is the chart of XRP/USD on the weekly time frame. Analyzing the market from the left, 0.20186 was the price from where the market roared to $3.29. Within a few months, the prices collapsed and held at 0.27923 for a year (September 2018 – September 2019). It finally broke below the support, bounced back from 0.17243, and went up to the support turned resistance area. The sellers came in quite strong from that area but could not successfully break below 0.17243 and make a lower low.

And thus, circled price action is nothing but a fake move. It, in fact, reacted from strong support made in mid-2017. These are all hints and clues that the sellers are fading out from business, and the buying is showings signs of strength. In the near future, levels of 0.27923 are very likely. And if that level again fails to make a lower low, the next target and area of concern would be 0.44863.

4. Chainlink Analysis

Fundamental Analysis

Chainlink is an Ethereum built decentralized oracle network. As the name suggests, the network is created to connect off-chain data sources like APIs, feeds, or bank transactions to the on-chain smart contract. This network came into the market in May 2019.

This platform comes with its own designed cryptocurrency LINK. The market capitalization of LINK currently stands at $1.52 billion, whose circulating supply is 350 million LINK tokens. The current price of LINK is only 12 percent down from the all-time highs within a year. Moreover, among the top 20 cryptocurrencies by market cap, LINK has turned out to be the best performer in 2019.

LINK features over 20 price oracles for Ethereum, which can be used for DeFi applications as an aggregated price source. It also offers price reference data, which is completely decentralized for several USD and ETH crypto pairs.

Technical Analysis

Below is the chat of LINK against the USD on the Daily time frame. The reason for choosing a smaller time frame is due to the fact that this coin is only a year old, and it is difficult to analyze the chart with lesser data. Reading the price action right from the beginning, it made a high to around $3 and retraced completely.

The market shot up again from the same area and managed to break above the previous high as well. Then, it came down to the area around $3.4, tried to make a new record high, failed, and rolled down to the first point of interest of the buyers. And yet again, the market reacted at this price started to move up. The $3.4 was a potential Support and Resistance level, but the sellers were unsuccessful in pushing the market down from that price.

In fact, the market held **above** the S&R area, indicating the weakness of the sellers. In a bird's eye view, we see the low is maintained, and the highs are getting higher and higher, as depicted in the chart. Therefore, the market is currently in the third leg to make a higher high. The minimum short-term target would be $6. And if the fundamentals continue to favor LINK, an up-trending market can be expected.

5. Tezos Analysis

Fundamental Analysis

Tezos is a decentralized smart contract and blockchain network that is linked to a digital currency, called Tez. The coin trades under the ticker XTZ. Tezos, unlike Bitcoin, is not based on mining, but the asset holders receive a reward for participating in the Proof-of-Stake consensus mechanism.

Tezos had an excellent start and a successful Initial Coin Offering (ICO) but was in problems due to delays and legal issues. However, it survived the crypto bear market, with its compelling Proof of Stake mechanism. Tezos is currently ranked 11th in CoinMarketCap based on market capitalization, which currently sums to $2.1 billion.

This coin was primarily created to solve the crippling government issues that have tormented Bitcoin and Ethereum previously. To date, three protocol upgrades — Athens, Babylon, and Carthage, have been put into play flawlessly. Fundamentals reflect a continuous increase in the daily transactions and active addresses in the past year.

Technical Analysis

Above is the chart of XTZ/USD on the 1D time frame. From the launch to the beginning of 2020, the Tezos prices had been moving in a range. In February 2020, the market finally broke above the resistance. After making an all-time high to around $4, it retraced to $2.49. The buyers did show up again but failed to make a higher high and also an equal high.

As a result, the market dropped all the way down to the point where the buyers made a higher high ($1.2000). The buyers did react from this area and even broke above $2.49 level. After the up move, it retraced and held above $2.49, signifying the strength of the buyers. Furthermore, comparing the price action with other cryptocurrencies, this coin has been trading above the support, while others are trading below it. Thus, in conclusion, the price is preparing to shoot north at least up to an all-time high.

Best Risk Management Techniques You Must Know

Why is Risk Management crucial?

Trading is a game of probabilities. In other words, a trading market is a place that is never certain. Thus, it comes with default risk. As a trader, the primary should be to reduce and manage risk the best way possible. In fact, professional traders believe that understanding risk management is more crucial than having a good strategy.

Going by the definition, risk refers to the probability of an event happening against the intended outcome. Trading involves making predictions between two choices. And risk in this domain is simply the percent of the money you are ready to lose. For instance, if the account balance of a trader is $1000 and he says he is risking 2% on a trade, it means that the trader is risking 2% of his account balance, which is $20. So, if the trade goes against the trader, he would be at most $20.

Risk Management Techniques

A trader who can manage their risk effectively can automatically maximize their profits. A professional traders' approach is to control their losses rather than running after profits. Here are some risk management strategies which mandatorily should be known by every trader.

1. Stop Loss and Take Profit

The first, foremost rule in trading is to have a stop loss and take profit for every trade. Stop-loss is an executable order that cuts the positions at a specified price when the market goes the intended direction. Take profit, on the other hand, is also an executable order than liquidates the positions when the market reaches a specified price in favor of the trader. A stop-loss will keep a trader safe from further losses and take profit will lock in the money even if the market goes against the desired direction later.

2. Position Sizing

Position sizing is the number of units of security invested by a trader. This is not a random number and is derived using the account size and risk tolerance.

Account risk

Firstly, account size is the account balance in a trading account. For example, if a trader deposits $1,000 into his trading account, then the account size will be $1,000.

Account risk is the percentage of the account size a trader is ready to lose on a trade. For example, if you set your account risk to 1%, then you will be risking 1% of your account balance on the trade.

Trade Risk

Trade risk is simply the stop loss for a trade. It is the difference between the entry price and the stop-loss price. For example, if the entry price for a buy is $210, and the stop loss is $160, the trade risk would be $50 per unit traded.

Position size

Using the above two parameters, the position size for a trade can be determined. Mathematically, the position size is obtained by dividing the account risk by the trade risk. For example, if the account risk on a trade is $100 and trade risk is $2 per unit, then position size would turn to be $100/$2 = 50 units.

3. Risk/Reward Ratio

Another important risk management tool is the risk/reward ratio. This ratio is the comparison of actual risk to the potential gains in a trade. The risk/reward tells you whether a trade is worth taking or not. For example, there could be situations when your stop loss has to be higher than the take profit. In such trades, you would be risking more than gaining.

Thus, this ratio is used to stay cautious with such scenarios. For instance, if a trader is risking $100 on a trade and the risk: reward is 1:1, then it means that he is risking $100 to make $100. Similarly, if the ratio was 1:2, then he would be risking $100 to make $200. Therefore, to safeguard your capital, it is advisable not to take any trades that are under 1:1.

Afterword

We hope you found this e-book informative and useful. It is crucial to know that the crypto markets are ever-changing. So the technical analysis that has been done may not be valid for a more extended period. But we made sure to suggest only those cryptos with strong fundamentals. Hence, even for the next couple of years, these cryptos will be an ideal crypto investment decision.

Having said that, please make sure to be due-diligent while making any investments in this space. If you are planning to invest a considerable sum of money, it is recommended to consult a financial advisor and act accordingly. Diversification is crucial in this space. If you find losses in a few cryptos, the others can save you.

Finally, we wish you a lot of profits and thank you for being a part of the unbelievable crypto revolution! Cheers!

www.ingramcontent.com/pod-product-compliance
Lightning Source LLC
Chambersburg PA
CBHW081104240526
45465CB00026B/3317